The American Flag

by Lisa M. Herrington

Content Consultant
Nanci R. Vargus, Ed.D.
Professor Emeritus, University of Indianapolis

Reading Consultant
Jeanne Clidas, Ph.D.
Reading Specialist

Children's Press®
An Imprint of Scholastic Inc.
New York Toronto London Auckland Sydney
Mexico City New Delhi Hong Kong
Danbury, Connecticut

Library of Congress Cataloging-in-Publication Data
Herrington, Lisa M.
The American flag/by Lisa M. Herrington.
     pages cm. — (Rookie read-about American symbols)
Includes bibliographical references and index.
ISBN 978-0-531-21566-1 (library binding: alk. paper) — ISBN 978-0-531-21839-6 (pbk.: alk. paper)
 1. Flags—United States—Juvenile literature. I. Title..

 CR113.H398 2014
 929.9'20973—dc23   2014014951

Produced by Spooky Cheetah Press
Design by Keith Plechaty

Printed in China 62

1 2 3 4 5 6 7 8 9 10 R 24 23 22 21 20 19 18 17 16 15

Photographs ©: Alamy Images/H. Mark Weidman Photography: 3 top right, 23, 28 right, 31 center bottom; Dreamstime/Vladimir Korostyshevskiy: 16, 31 bottom; Getty Images: 12 (Christian Aslund), 8 (Mitchell Funk), 19 (MPI), 24 (Vito Palmisano); Media Bakery: 7, 29 (Ariel Skelley), 3 bottom (Blend Images), 4 (Richard T. Nowitz); NASA: 27; Newscom/Rich Graessle/Icon SMI CGV: 20, 31 center top; The Granger Collection: 11, 28 left, 31 top; Thinkstock: 3 top left (Bosphorus), cover (Stockbyte); Wikimedia/Carl Lindberg: 15.

Map by XNR Productions, Inc.: p. 30

Table of Contents

Stars and Stripes Forever

The American flag is one of the most important **symbols** of the United States. It flies near schools and government buildings. People hang it outside their homes. We honor it at sports games. We wave it proudly on the Fourth of July.

The flag flies in front of the U.S. Capitol Building in Washington, D.C.

The American flag stands for the land and the people of the United States of America. It also stands for freedom.

The first U.S. flag became official on June 14, 1777. Each year, Americans celebrate Flag Day on June 14.

FUN FACT!

Our flag has different names. It is sometimes called the Stars and Stripes.

The colors of the American flag are red, white, and blue. The flag has 50 white stars on a blue background. They stand for the 50 states that make up our country. There are 13 stripes— seven red and six white. They stand for the 13 states that first formed our country.

FUN FACT!

The flag colors have meaning. Red is for courage. White is for goodness. Blue is for fairness.

A Changing Symbol

America was once ruled by Great Britain. More than 200 years ago, Americans fought for **independence**. The United States became its own country. It needed a flag.

FUN FACT!

A rattlesnake appeared on some early American flags. It was chosen because a rattlesnake is deadly when attacked.

The first flag had 13 stars and 13 stripes. They stood for the 13 colonies that later became the first 13 states. Some people think Betsy Ross of Philadelphia sewed the first flag. No one really knows for sure.

This painting shows Betsy Ross and her helpers making the first American flag.

Vermont and Kentucky then joined the United States. In 1795, two stars and two stripes were added to the flag. It now had 15 stars and 15 stripes.

The 15-star flag was the second official U.S. flag.

15

What would happen as more states joined the country? The flag could get very crowded. In 1818, lawmakers decided it would have 13 stripes. A new star would be added for each state.

There was no rule on how the stars should be placed, however. Some flags had the stars in rows. Others had them in circles. In 1912, President Taft decided they should be in rows. Over the years, more stars were added as more states joined the country.

William Howard Taft was America's 27th president.

19

Pride in the Flag

Americans honor the flag in many ways. They sing "The Star-Spangled Banner" to show their pride. That is America's **national anthem**, a special song written to celebrate the flag.

The crowd at a baseball game stands for the national anthem.

Many kids say a **pledge** to the flag at the start of the school day. It is called the Pledge of Allegiance. The pledge is a promise to be loyal to the United States.

FUN FACT!

Francis Bellamy wrote the Pledge of Allegiance. It first appeared in a children's magazine in 1892.

The Flag Today

Today, there are different rules to care for the flag. For example, the flag should never touch the ground. It should not fly in bad weather unless it is waterproof. If the flag is flown at night, it should have a light shining on it.

This flag is part of the Iwo Jima Memorial, in Arlington, Virginia.

After Hawaii became a state in 1959, another star was added to the flag. Since then, the American flag has flown proudly with 50 stars.

Whenever people see the American flag, they think of the United States—the land of the free.

FUN FACT!

In 1969, two U.S. astronauts became the first people on the moon. They flew an American flag there.

1814
Lawyer Francis Scott Key writes "The Star-Spangled Banner."

1892
The Pledge of Allegiance is first published in a children's magazine.

1777
The first official U.S. flag has 13 stars and 13 stripes.

1818
A new law says the flag will have 13 stripes and a star for each state.

1949
Flag Day is made a national holiday.

1960
The 50th star is added to the flag.

1969
U.S. astronauts fly the American flag on the moon.

Today
The 50-star flag still flies proudly.

Adding Stars to the Flag

Canada

Rhode Island 1790
New Hampshire 1788
Vermont 1791
Massachusetts 1788
Connecticut 1788
Maine 1820

Washington 1889
Montana 1889
North Dakota 1889
Minnesota 1858
New York 1788

Oregon 1859
Idaho 1890
Wisconsin 1848
Michigan 1837
Pennsylvania 1787
New Jersey 1787

Wyoming 1890
Iowa 1846
Ohio 1803

Nevada 1864
Utah 1896
Colorado 1876
Nebraska 1867
Illinois 1818
Indiana 1816
West Virginia 1863
Virginia 1788
Delaware 1787

California 1850
Kansas 1861
Missouri 1821
Kentucky 1792
North Carolina 1789
Maryland 1788

Arizona 1912
New Mexico 1912
Oklahoma 1907
Arkansas 1836
Tennessee 1796
South Carolina 1788

Texas 1845
Alabama 1819
Mississippi 1817
Louisiana 1812
Georgia 1788
Florida 1845

Atlantic Ocean

Gulf of Mexico

Pacific Ocean

Mexico

Hawaii 1959

Alaska 1959

MAP KEY

United States

Georgia 1788 — State name and year it was added to the United States

This map shows when each state joined the United States.

Find where you live on the map. What year was your state added to the United States? Is there a state that was added before yours? Can you find one that was added after? Were any states added in the same year?

Glossary

independence (in-di-PEN-duhnss): freedom

national anthem (NASH-uh-nuhl AN-thum): a country's official song

pledge (PLEJ): a promise

symbols (SIM-buhls): objects or designs that stand for something else

Index

Facts for Now

Visit this Scholastic Web site for more information on the American flag:

www.factsfornow.scholastic.com

Enter the keywords **American Flag**

About the Author

Lisa M. Herrington writes books and articles for kids. She feels proud whenever she sees the American flag. Lisa lives in Trumbull, Connecticut, with her husband, Ryan, and daughter, Caroline.